AF368775

Michael O. Amamieye

A MIRACLE Will Settle your CASE

Published by:

Michael Amamieye Word Outreach, International

a/k/a Aggressive Faith Ministries

Plot 13 Walter Akpana Lay Out

Off 394 Ikwerre Road Mile 5 Rumueprikom

P. O. Box 12378, Port Harcourt, Nigeria.

E-mail: info@aggressivefaith.org

Web site: www.aggressivefaith.org

Phone: +234-9018006296, +2348050987377

+1-916-245-6157 (U.S.A.)

WhatsApp: +234-8036732188.

ISBN: 978-33230-0-8-007

Printed in the Federal Republic of Nigeria

WARNING!

This book alongside your
Bible is the final blow
To the onslaughts of
Satan, sickness and sorrow.

You can't help but
experience real
Miracles from today!

This book is lovingly
Dedicated to:

Mehetabel Favour

Baby you are a miracle that settled my case…mummy and I love you so much!

SONG

1. Jesus of Nazareth

A man approved of God

With signs, wonders & miracles

Is here right now

In His name.

2. Jesus Christ

Anointed by God our Father

With the Holy Ghost & power

To do you good

Call on Him

Refrain

A miracle will settle your case

Once and for all

A miracle will settle your case

Only believe

©1998 Michael O. Amamieye

CONTENTS

PREFACE

In 1989 when I was ordained into the work of the ministry, the Lord gave me a sound and definite mandate to my generation. He said, ***"Son, take this gospel and miracle power of the risen Christ to the nations - impacting lives and destinies with the WORD!"*** That was the word that carried me into full time world evangelism. By that word, it became evident that I shall carry the miracle working grace of God across the land and ***"... also from sea to sea, and from the river unto the ends of the earth."*** Psalm 72:8.

The Lord has assured me that in my days. I ***"...shall the righteous flourish..."*** and they shall have ***"... abundance of peace so long as the moon endures."*** Psalm 72:7.

I was born for the fulfillment of this scripture in your life. The yoke of oppression shall be broken in pieces over your life in the name of Jesus Christ. Amen.

As I travel around the nations of the earth preaching this gospel, I am seeing the yoke destroying power of God's word change many lives. The power of the word broke the yoke of prayerlessness in the life of one of my friends in Ireland. After reading one of my messages, he sent in this testimony: *"Bishop Amamieye, thanks again for your power filled messages. I am praying everyday now."* Wow! That is what the word can do.

As you read this book, I hear the sound of abundance of rain. The rain is coming!

The heaven will pour down rain on your life and concerns. Rain is symbolic of revival, revolution and release of your harvests. I remember preaching at the Creekview Assembly of God Church in Amherst, New York in 2001. I preached a prophetic word on ***Lord, Send The Rain***. It was during the fall season when they had not seen rain for some time. The leaves had turned brown.

As I was screaming inside the church building, ***Lord, send the rain***. The heavens literally opened and it rained heavily. God honored the word of His prophet with a physical sign. I have seen this happened several times. That is why I am very confident that it will happen to you as you read on. Get your house ready because the rain is coming on you. Revival is coming to every dead dream, marriage, ministry and finances. Revolution is coming into the system just to favor you. Release is coming because it is your time for a change.

You will flourish and prosper where you have failed before now. God will bring you to a rest. This rest is freedom from worry and fear; freedom from sickness and disease; freedom from guilt and condemnation. You will come to know true liberty in Jesus name. Amen.

In more than thirty years of world evangelism, I see this mandate impact lives and destinies in five continents so far. Through the simple proclamation of the gospel of Jesus Christ, hardened criminals, prostitutes, drug addicts, etc, are translated from darkness to light. What a miracle!

It was after preaching this same gospel in one of our local crusades in Warri, Delta State of Nigeria that a notable criminal surrendered his life to Christ. As I took my seat, one of the two first class chiefs who represented the king told me, *'Rev. Mike, if this is the only thing this crusade accomplished, it is worth it.'*

A young man in his twenties had suffered from schizophrenia, a multiple personality disorder, and drug addiction. He was in a terrible state when my healing service got to his city in Cleveland, Ohio. His mother brought him to the service expecting a miracle. This young man was healed the first night by the power of the spoken word. He was literally delivered completely from drugs and schizophrenia. There is power, miracle-working power in the gospel.

"For I am not ashamed of the gospel of Christ: for it is the power of God unto salvation to every one that believeth; to the Jew first, and also to the Greek." Romans 1:16.

Get ready for a miracle!

Through this message, the miracle grace of God on my life is flowing to you in a special way. Receive it by faith and watch the Holy Spirit overshadow you as He manifests that miracle that will settle your case forever!

"So Apollos and I should be looked upon as Christ's servants who distribute God's blessings by explaining God's secrets."

1 Corinthians 4:1. (The Living Bible).

My job is just to explain His secrets to you. As I am doing this, guess what is happening? He is distributing His blessings to you. What is a blessing to you? It can be salvation for your soul or for a loved one. It can be healing of all sickness and disease. It can be deliverance from a life style that has enslaved you for years. It can be freedom from bad habits, hurts and hang-ups. These blessings are what we call miracles! Wow! It is this simple. Receive His miracles as you read His secrets in this book. Expect miracles!

Introduction

Life is in stages. Each stage of life has its peculiar challenge that faces each person. No human being is free from the divers' challenges of life. Sometimes when you look at some people, you think they don't have any problems at all. So, you wish, if I am like so and so, all my troubles will be over. God help you when you become so and so in terms of occupying their office or position, you will realize that the office or position has its peculiar challenges that you wish you can brush under the carpet. The bottom line is that every human being born into this world will have troubles to deal with. Real people with real troubles.

"Man that is born of a woman is of few days, and full of trouble."

Job 14:1.

At different points and phases of life, we are faced with situations that defy our native sense and intelligence. We find ourselves in real situations that we call *"a fix"* not because we are fixed or established but for the fact that what we have as a beautiful dream has hit some unseen rocks. It is a situation of dream shipwreck. Our dream ship that was smooth sailing has suddenly sunk into some sandy shallow spot.

You will agree with me that at such times you get pushed to an invisible wall that puts a limit to your progressive movement. Yes, indeed, you are pressured on every side to the point where it is as if you have come to the end of the road. Medical science becomes blank and slow in diagnosing the real situation. Since no diagnosis is reached, it becomes clearly written on the wall of your soul that this particular case is hopeless. Even the geographers are not left out, as they cannot find a way out. The navigators can't find a direction.

I want you to realize that if you are faced with any situation that makes you feel so helpless and probably lose hope, you are not alone. You are not the first and you will not be the last. The great apostle Paul said:

"I think you ought to know, dear brothers and sisters, about the trouble we went through in the province of Asia. We were crushed and completely overwhelmed, and we thought we would never live through it."

2 Cor. 1:8. (New Living Translation).

Can you believe that even this great man of God was troubled to the point that he gave up hope of surviving? This is a real situation where normally if you add one and one together, you must get two anywhere in the world. But at such times it seems to be that one plus one is giving you three or four or more. You are confused not knowing what to do or where to turn to for help.

Of course, there is the very heavy temptation to look up to friends, family members and colleagues only to be greatly disappointed.

It is my personal discovery that at such times real friends do not appear to be the same people we call friends. I cannot explain it but it is the fact. There is something in you that attract people to you whom you call friends. When that thing is gone they simply disappear too. Basically, if there is a prospect that you will become somebody, those who see it want to befriend you early enough. When you eventually become they just flow to you.

"The poor is hated even of his neighbour; but the rich hath many friends." Prov.14:20.

"Wealth maketh many friends; but the poor is separated from his neighbour." Prov.19:4.

The most unfortunate part is that when we find ourselves in crisis situations the last place we get to is supposed to be the first: **GOD!** God happens to be the last resort when all else has failed and disappointed us.

Always remember that Jehovah God holds the key to the door you are trying to open with your fingers. No matter how good your finger is, it can't open that door for you. You need the key. You need a miracle. A miracle will settle the matter once and for all eternity.

I will never forget after the Lord Jesus appeared to me sometime in 1988, He told me clearly: *'Son, I have empowered the words of your mouth'*. Those words shot straight into the deepest recesses of my being like a bullet. It hit right home. The next morning, my dear friend, Mike Aloko, brought a man whose case was considered hopeless. He had three situations: one, his brain was turned upside down so that if you tell him to go what his brain translates was come. He was such a mess that even his children made fun of him.

As if that was not enough, the devil blew his eardrum that kept producing wax. As if that was still not enough embarrassment, the Devil planted a growth in his stomach. That Devil is a bad Devil. He is wicked. I hate him with every fiber of my being and I have vowed to frustrate him until he bows his knees in total surrender to the Lordship of my Lord and Master Jesus Christ. Amen.

By the power of the spoken word imparted into my being that early morning, I told that man to stand away from me while I spoke words loaded with the creative force of God's divine nature. Those words were not mere words but words that carried the miracle that settled that man's case. And the miracles took place one after the other. First, his brain was turned right side up. Alleluyah!

Next, a brand new eardrum replaced the damaged one. When he went for a checkup, the doctors told him that he had a new eardrum like that of a newborn child. What a miracle! Finally, the growth first moved up. I was not satisfied. I commanded it to leave and it left the man's body. That man is a living evidence that the days of miracles are not over yet. He is a proof that only a miracle will settle your case once and for all eternity. As we go on, get ready for a miracle that will re-write your story in life.

The biggest lie you were ever told is that your own situation is hopeless. Medically, it may be. But a miracle will settle the issue. In fact, I like the word hopeless now. If you split into two, you have: hope and less. It means there is hope but it is less. In a situation like this, all you need is to connect with the God of hope and He will fill you with so much hope that you become hopeful.

"Now the God of hope fill you with all joy and peace in believing, that ye may abound in hope, through the power of the Holy Ghost."

Rom. 15:13.

Many years ago doctors found it difficult operating on patients with situations like growth, tumors, cancer and other conditions that require operation. Today, the situation has improved. There are conditions that were terminal years ago that have solutions today. One time I was at the Indian High Commission to get a visa to go to India, most of the visa applicants I saw there were going for medical treatment. It seems like India has some of the best procedures and practices that solves a lot of medical problems that Nigerian doctors are still trying to find solution for.

There was a time when operations were dreaded because of the pains associated with it. The doctors did not know that they could put their patient to sleep before the procedure in order to avoid the pain. One day, someone discovered why the first operation in the Bible was successful. In Genesis 2:21,22, when God operated on Adam to take out Eve, He had to put Adam to sleep first before He carried out that operation. Just right there was the secret to an ageless hopeless case: anesthesia. It has always been there but was only recently discovered. No wonder they say that science is a discovery. It is a discovery of what God has covered.

What you call hopeless has been covered by God Himself. It becomes a miracle when you discover it. That is why you should not accept that lie from anyone that your case is hopeless. There is a way out of every mess you find yourself. There is a way out of every mistake you have found yourself. There is a way out of every fix. A miracle will chart the course, show the way and settle the case!

Chapter One

Miracles still happen

A miracle is a supernatural interference in naturally difficult situations. It is a divine intervention in seemingly impossible cases. It is God's panacea for your problems.

When a man is dying in sin, he is conscious of the weight of the consequences of sin which ends in death, that is, eternal separation from God in hell. Just as he is about to slip into hell, he becomes born again. He becomes translated from the kingdom of darkness into the kingdom of light. Joy unspeakable floods his life to know that his sins are forever forgiven and that he is on his way to heaven. Just when he is about to slip into eternal darkness, there was an interception from God that changed his eternal destination. That is a miracle!

That was the case of Nicole, a young woman who was invited to one of my miracle meetings. After I finished preaching the simple gospel, she came out all by herself weeping. Her breath smelt cigarette. I asked her what she wanted and her response was that she wanted to be saved. She knew she was a sinner with distinction and she could not help herself. I led her to Christ and prayed for her. The miracle took place immediately as she busted in unspeakable joy. Even after the service was over she was so overwhelmed with joy that she said she could not stop the laughter that was exploding from her belly. Wow! That was the joy of salvation.

"In the last day, that great day of the feast, Jesus stood and cried, saying, If any man thirst, let him come unto me, and drink.

He that believeth on me, as the scripture hath said, out of his belly shall flow rivers of living water.

(But this spake he of the Spirit, which they that believe on him should receive: for the Holy

Ghost was not yet given; because that Jesus was not yet glorified.)" John 7:37-39.

Nicole was radically transformed and filled with joy unspeakable. That is what a miracle is about. It brings a radical change in hopeless situations. It brings a radical transformation in hopeless people. It changes those that society has written off.

Friend, it takes a miracle to translate a chronic sinner to a changed saint in heart and attitude. Only a miracle can transform a night crawler to a light bearer.

You will agree with me that habits are easy to cultivate but difficult to conquer. Only a miracle can break that bad habit you have been struggling to overcome.

That reminds me of a man I witnessed to sometime in 1984. He was so convinced to the point of accepting Jesus into his heart when he broke down and said that his only problem was smoking. He was literally addicted to cigar. I told him that I could pray for him and that cigar will become his worst enemy. He thought it was a joke. I prayed for him, took his address and let him go. The next day I was at his place towards the evening time. He was so astounded that he came before me shaking like a leaf to welcome me into his house. And, that was his opportunity. He became born again.

A miracle broke a habit he could not conquer. New Year resolutions could not resolve it. What is that bad habit that you have been struggling with? Is it sex, eating disorder, gambling, masturbation or stealing? Whatever it is, you can be free. A miracle will settle your case in Jesus name. Amen.

"Now there cried a certain woman of the wives of the sons of the prophets unto Elisha, saying, Thy servant my husband is dead; and thou knowest that thy servant did fear the LORD:

2 Kings 4:1.

This woman was in a situation like someone reading this book. Her situation was so bad. The husband who was the breadwinner of the family was dead. I suspect that when the husband was alive, he must have borrowed to maintain his family. Now that he was dead, the creditors came threatening to take her two sons to be slaves. What a tragedy!

She was bereaved. She was in debt that she could not pay. As if that was not enough she was faced with the fact of losing her two sons. Sons they say have a promising future that is why in most cultures, a woman is not complete if she is unable to have at least a son. That is only cultural because children are a reward from God and they have great future whether they be sons or daughters.

This woman's situation calls for a miracle. Only a miracle will answer the creditor at the door. Only a miracle will change the story. Only a miracle will remove the shame and reproach left behind by her dead husband.

What is it that has died around you? Have you lost a loved one? Have you lost a promising business or career? Have you lost that job that gave you the hope of keeping your body and soul together? Have you lost your home? Just like that, it's all gone? Whatever it is that you have lost, there is hope. I am so sure that you are reading this book right now because God has scheduled a miracle for you that will change your story.

A miracle will settle your case!

Are you in debt? It may be so bad that you are almost thinking of committing suicide. Is your life and property coming under severe threats by your creditors? Are you just about to lose some of your cherished treasures? Have you received threat notes and letters from the underworld or hit men? Before you lose your mind and everything, God has sent me with a word that can change your story for good.

A word from God can alter your destiny permanently.

What you need is a miracle. The miracle factor will alter your condition. A miracle will settle the matter!

My joy and confidence is in the fact that the God of heaven whom I serve is The Miracle Worker. He is the custodian and monopolist of real miracles. He has done it before. He will do it again. He did it for men and women, boys and girls in the Bible. He has done it for many real people in our days. He will do it for you today.

*"Jesus Christ the same yesterday, and to day,
and for ever."*

Heb. 13:8.

Some people have said that the days of miracles are over. It only tickles me because I am a witness of the fact that miracles are for now. My life story is a track record of miracles from the day I was conceived until this day. I cannot tell you all my miracles because they are in volumes of unprinted pages.

How can I tell you how I conquered almost thirty million contestants to lay hold of the trophy, I mean the egg, in my mother's womb? At that state where I knew nothing but I made it. The proof is evident. That is a miracle! No wonder the conception of a human being in the womb of a woman is a miracle indeed.

How can I tell you what I was doing in my mother's womb for nine solid and long months? I don't remember a thing but I am alive and well. Millions died and never saw the light of day. But I am alive to give proof that miracles are for now.

How can I tell of how I survived those six deadly killer diseases without the aid of vaccines? I never knew that this world is full of viruses and germs that hate my existence. But I am alive and well to give proof that miracles still happen!

Miracles did not die with the last apostle. I am living evidence miracles still happen!

How can I tell you how that my father was killed in his prime just when I needed him most as a child? I was starved. In fact, I was ripped off of a father's love, care and discipline. Every child needs a father to impart the correction and discipline that will ensure a good future. I was deprived of it yet my future is sure. It is as sure as the noonday. The plan of the enemy was to render my life useless but I am alive today giving fatherly love, care and discipline to others. I am a proof of the fact that miracles still happen!

I can go on telling you my miracles but I don't want to because of space. I trust that one day, I will be able to print them in volumes for the generations to come.

Miracles still happen! In 2008, while ministering in Lome, Togo, a child died. The mother was in the service. So the dead child was carried to the church. My host took the dead child and placed him on top of one of the box speakers in order not to distract me. As I kept preaching the word, the power of the word went into the body of the dead child. That child came alive by the power of the spoken word. Even the dead are coming alive literally. Who told you the days of miracles are over? They lied to you. Miracles still happen!

I believe that doubt is gradually dissolving from your heart about the reality of miracles today. A miracle will re-write your story!

What you read in the Bible can happen to you because Jesus Christ is the same yesterday, today and forever. He has not changed. He is the same miracle working Jesus of the Bible. He is alive today as He was those days. He is here where you are reading this book. He is there with you right now.

"Jesus Christ the same yesterday, and to day, and for ever."

Hebrews 13:8.

Chapter Two

SEEK THE MIRACLE WORKER

Miracles have changed my life every step of the way. I love God for who He is to me. He is the miracle I need. He told Abraham when papa Abby cried, *"…what wilt thou give me, seeing I go childless…"* God said, *"… I am thy shield, and thy exceeding great reward."* Gen. 15:1,2.

In essence, God said to Abraham, I am the child you need. I am everything you need. Do you need a wife? He says, I am the wife you need. Do you need a husband? He says, I am your husband. *"For thy maker is thine husband…"* Isa. 54:5.

"….as the bridegroom rejoiceth over the bride, so shall thy God rejoice over thee".

Isa. 62:5.

"Turn, O backsliding children, saith the Lord; for I am married unto you…" Jere. 3:14.

I was at Bori in Ogoni land in 1993 for one of my meetings when a woman who felt she was passed the age of getting married came to my hotel room. I gave her a few doses of the above scriptures. And, I prayed for her for her miracle husband to manifest. I was there the following year when she ran to me so excitedly asking if I do remember her. She went on to tell me how the miracle took place that same year as she was happily married. It can happen to you today. Seek the miracle worker. Are you childless and you are being mocked? God is saying, I am your children.

"Sing, O barren, thou that didst not bear; break forth into singing, and cry aloud thou that didst not travail with child: for more are the children of the desolate than the children of the married wife, saith the LORD."

Isa. 54:1.

Did you hear what The Miracle Worker said? He said, YOUR CHILDREN ARE MORE! Alleluia! That calls for celebration. Put on your dancing shoes and get down celebrating your miracle. If the miracle worker said it, you can take it to the bank. His word is a check that does not bounce. Yes, His word is collateral that guarantees the reality of your miracle.

You need to read I Samuel 1 and see what Hannah went through just because she was childless. She was ridiculed by her mate. Yet, it was this same Hannah who gave birth to one of the greatest prophets and in fact the last Judge in Israel besides the other three sons and two daughters she had. This was her own testimony: *"...the barren hath born seven...."* I Sam. 2:5.

This revelation changed the life of Abraham so that later when Isaac asked, *"... Behold the fire and the wood: but where is the lamb for a burnt offering?"* Abraham's answer was pointed and sharp as he said, *"...my son, God will provide himself a lamb for a burnt offering..."* Gen. 22:7,8.

Abraham spoke the language of faith when he said, *God will provide Himself as a lamb for the burnt offering.*

Next time if somebody asks you, where is your capital for the business? Tell them, the Lord will provide Himself as my capital for the business in Jesus name. Amen. If you are asked, where is your house? Tell them, the Lord will provide Himself as my house in Jesus name. Amen.

The Lord will provide Himself... is now your answer to those questions. He has made up His mind to turn Himself to meet your need no matter the shape or size. He is the sovereign Lord. He has the prerogative and ability to turn Himself to anything since He created all things.

If witches can turn to rats, cockroaches, etc., how much more the Creator of the universe. Remember that everything we see came out of Him. They express an aspect of His Person. He can become anything just to reach you where you are. That is why I challenge you to seek God not His blessings. If you get the Blesser, you have got the blessings. It is that easy and automatic.

Seek the miracle Maker and you contact His miracles. Even if you lose the miracle, because you have the miracle worker He can always make the miracles happen.

"And ye shall know the truth, and the shall make you free."

John 8:32.

I want to remind you that the TRUTH is a Person, a real Person.   He said, I am the

TRUTH. John 14:6. Jesus is The Truth. He also said, ***"And ye shall know the truth, and the truth [that you know] shall make you free."*** To know means to be well informed of; to interact with personally.

Seek to interact with the miracle worker personally and He shall MAKE you free. He did not say that He shall set you free. He is the MAKER. That is exciting! Whatever miracle I have missed in the past, He can MAKE it happen again. That is the God of a second and third and fourth chance.

He is the WAY MAKER where there was no way. He is the LIGHT in a dark and lonely path. He is my PEACE in the midst of the storm. He is the miracle I need now. His miracle will settle your case… Get ready!

"And Moses said unto God, Behold, when I come unto the children of Israel, and shall say unto them, The God of your fathers hath sent

*me unto you; and they shall say to me, What is
his name? what shall I say unto them?*

*And God said unto Moses, I AM THAT I AM:
and he said, Thus shalt thou say unto the
children of Israel, I AM hath sent me unto
you."*

Exodus 3:13,14.

*"And God said to Moses, I AM WHO I AM and
WHAT I AM, and I WILL BE WHAT I WILL
BE; and He said, You shall say this to the
Israelites: I AM has sent me to you!"*

Exodus 3:14. (Amplified Version.)

Chapter Three

STOP COMPLAINING

"Now there cried a certain woman of the wives of the sons of the prophets unto Elisha, saying, Thy servant my husband is dead; and thou knowest that thy servant did fear the LORD: and the creditor is come to take unto him my two sons to be bondmen."

2 Kings 4:1.

The woman in our story knew WHO to run to for a miracle. Miracles happen when you know WHO to run to in times of trouble. Let this sink into your soul and spirit.

She cried to a man of God even though crying did not solve her problem. That is to tell us that not all cries bring about heaven's intervention. Some people use their cries to manipulate and control people of weak minds just like children do at times.

Some children use this weapon of strong cries to intimidate and pressure their parents to do what they want. They wait until maybe when visitors are around so that if they cry it will cause an embarrassment to their parents. To avoid the embarrassment, the parents will quickly give them what they ask.

When we come to God, we want to use the same method with the hope that we can manipulate Him. But God is not a man. ***"God is not a man..."*** Num. 23:19. He cannot be manipulated. In fact, such cries and fears are offensive to Him.

"And this have ye done again, covering the altar of the LORD with tears, with weeping, and with crying out, insomuch that he regardeth not the offering any more, or receiveth it with good will at your hand."

Mal. 2:13.

Friend, as good as crying is to your being, it does not improve your situation. It may help you as you cry out the pressure but it doesn't help your situation.

Crying, whining, grinding and murmuring will not improve your situation at all. Murmuring and complaining brings God's judgement.

"Neither murmur ye, as some of them also murmured, and were destroyed of the destroyer."

I Cor. 10:10.

Every time you murmur, you open the door for the destroyer to destroy you.

So, stop murmuring!

Stop worrying!

But Brother Mike, how can I not be bothered when my child is dying and there is no money to even admit him in the hospital? How can I not be worried when I don't know how to get the house rent before my landlord throws me out of his house?

That is exactly what Sherri asked me when her car ran into her neighbor's garage. She thought she had insurance only to discover that her insurance was not valid. She was worried on how she would cough out several thousands of dollars to fix the neighbors garage and car. I told her severally, stop worrying. She asked me, how can I not be worried? Finally, I said to her, let us pray for a miracle. The miracle happened. Her insurance company took responsibility. What a relief!

I know that these are real situations that happen to real people like you and me. But let us face facts. Since you started worrying, what help have you received?

If the Master of the universe says that you should not worry don't you think that He must be up to something? For the fact that Jesus said it three consecutive times should settle the matter once and for all in your heart. This is what Jesus said:

"Therefore I say unto you, take no thought for your life, what ye shall eat, or what ye shall drink: nor yet for your body, what ye shall put on...

Which of you by taking thought can add one cubit unto his stature? And why take ye thought for raiment?

Therefore take no thought, saying, what shall we eat? Or what shall we drink? Or, wherewithal shall we be clothed?

Take therefore no thought for the morrow: for the morrow shall take thought for the things of itself."

Matt. 6:25,27,31,34.

Have you made a mistake and you are regretting about it? Regrets have never recalled any event before. Instead of regretting, repent before God in honesty and sincerity of heart.

"Now I rejoice, not that ye were made sorry, but that ye sorrowed to repentance: for ye were made sorry after a godly manner...

For godly sorrow worketh repentance to salvation not to be repented of: but the sorrow of the world worketh death."

2 Cor. 7:9,10.

When she cried to the man of God, Elisha did not sympathize with her. Sympathy doesn't meet needs. Stop looking for sympathy. Stop giving it to people because it never solves the problem.

Only compassion can change a man's situation.

Compassion creates a very conducive atmosphere for miracles.

Compassion is divine love in motion. It is a situation where you are moved by the love of God to reach out to someone in pains, needs, etc. Jesus' ministry was distinguished and noised abroad by compassion. Anytime He was moved by compassion, miracles happened.

"And Jesus went forth, and saw a great multitude, and was moved with compassion towards them, and He healed their sick."

Matt.14:14.

"So Jesus had compassion on them, and touched their eyes: and immediately their eyes received sight, and they followed him."

Matt. 20:34.

I will never forget how a dear friend of mine, an army colonel, was saved from being killed in 1991. I just led this man to Christ and started using his house for fellowship twice a week. One day when I got to the house, at the gate, the wife ran to me crying that her husband had been whisked away by state security service men. His offence was that someone had implicated him in the Gideon Orka coup that failed.

As soon as I heard the news, I was moved from the deepest recesses of my being and I spoke a word that he shall not die but live to give proof to the existence of my God. That word shot into the atmosphere and became a covering for my friend.

After three months, he came out alive to share his testimony. This is a man who was in the army for twenty-six solid years. When he was arrested, he was taken to a place he never knew was in existence in this country. That was a place where men were led to the slaughter like sheep on a regular basis. The day he was to be executed, an army major was assigned the job. As soon as the major saw him, he exclaimed *'Oga na you!'* This major had served under this man and enjoyed him.

That is why it pays to be good.

The good you do to someone today is a seed that you will eventually reap tomorrow.

The major told him that he was assigned to waste him. Thank God who is the Master arranger. By the prophetic word from the bowels of compassion, God arranged it so. That was how my friend was saved. Today he is alive and well to give proof of God's miracle. Miracles will happen where there is compassion.

Someone might be wondering how this works. Judges 4:4 tells us that Deborah was a prophetess who judged Israel at a time in the history of Israel. She called Barak to lead the army of Israel to war against Jabin who ruled Canaan the Promised Land. Barak did not have the courage to go to war unless Deborah went with him. That day, Deborah spoke into the atmosphere:

"And Barak said unto her, If thou wilt go with me, then I will go: but if thou wilt not go with me, then I will not go.

And she said, I will surely go with thee: notwithstanding the journey that thou takest shall not be for thine honour; for the LORD shall sell Sisera into the hand of a woman. And Deborah arose, and went with Barak to Kedesh."

Judges 4:8,9.

Her word was that God was going to deliver the head of Sisera captain of Jabin's army into the hand of a woman. Watch what that word did: the stars of heaven which are angelic beings took the words of this prophetess and fought Sisera.

"They fought from heaven; the stars in their courses fought against Sisera." Judges 5:20.

The result was that Sisera was killed eventually by a little woman. This was the miracle result of a prophetic word.

"Howbeit Sisera fled away on his feet to the tent of Jael the wife of Heber the Kenite: for there was peace between Jabin the king of Hazor and the house of Heber the Kenite.

Then Jael Heber's wife took a nail of the tent, and took an hammer in her hand, and went softly unto him, and smote the nail into his temples, and fastened it into the ground: for he was fast asleep and weary. So he died.

And, behold, as Barak pursued Sisera, Jael came out to meet him, and said unto him, Come, and I will shew thee the man whom thou seekest. And when he came into her tent, behold, Sisera lay dead, and the nail was in his temples."

Judges 4:17, 21,22.

Miracles happen when a prophetic word is spoken over your life, marriage, finances, ministry, etc. Sometimes what will cause the miracles to happen is a word from God's prophets sent to your life. A word of blessing spoken over your life by your pastor or parent or prophet will change your situation. Expect miracles!

Chapter Four

WHAT DO YOU HAVE?

Anytime you move in His love, miracles will happen. Most of the time when we need miracles, we come asking God to do it again. We cry, *'God do this for me. God do that for me.'* The woman came crying to Elisha for a miracle. I thought that Elisha would have jumped up and begin to storm the gate of heaven as most ministers are likely to do. I thought that he would have called on the God of Elijah his former boss to send fire to consume the creditors for troubling this poor widow.

"And Elisha said unto her, What shall I do for thee? tell me, what hast thou in the house…?"

2 Kings 4:2.

O, come on Elisha, how can you ask this poor widow these silly questions? I thought with the double anointing of Elijah, you would just roll out five syllables of tongues and speak a word of miracle.

No, he did not do that.

Rather, he said, woman I cannot help you but if you HAVE something a miracle can happen. The apostle Paul talked about the gift of **"...the working of miracles..."** I Cor. 12:10.

The word, **working**, is also translated as **processing** in another version. Miracles are processed or worked. They go through a process. That means you can create your miracles with a point of contact. Your miracle is spiritual but you need it in this physical realm. There must be a point of contact between the spiritual and physical planes. By the law of contact and transmission when a point of contact is established there will be a transmission, a transfer or transfusion.

What do you HAVE to release your miracle?

Moses had a rod when God met him on the mount called Horeb. As Moses argued with God that the Israelites will not believe him, God asked *him "...What is in thine hand? And he said, A rod."* Ex. 3:2.

God used Moses' rod to work miracles. The rod turned to snake that swallowed Pharaoh's snakes. The rod turned the river Nile into blood. The rod brought frogs from the river that the Egyptians could not handle. The rod brought flies, animal diseases, boils, hails, locusts and thick darkness in Egypt.

With the rod, Moses parted the Red Sea. He brought water out of the rock with the rod.

It seems to me that there was no limit to what that rod could do. I can assure you that if Moses wanted to make the job faster, all he needed to do would have been to hit Pharaoh with this miracle rod and Pharaoh would have just disappeared.

It made miracles easy for Moses.

There is something you HAVE right now that God can use to work miracles ceaselessly in your life.

The woman of Zarephath had only a meal for one person. I Kings 17. She could have eaten it and died in famine. But when she let go of it, she ate until the famine was over.

The woman in our text had just a pot of oil.

The point is that it is not how little or insignificant what you HAVE is. It is not how much or how great.

It is that you HAVE something at all.

And, you HAVE something right now. What you HAVE can be turned into a miracle for you. It is what you do with what you HAVE that God will use to prosper you. What you HAVE will become the raw material for the processing of your miracle.

What you HAVE will create the atmosphere for your miracle.

"A gift is as a precious stone in the eyes of him that hath it: withersoever it turneth, it prospereth."

Prov. 17:8.

Let what you HAVE be very precious and valuable in your eyes. Let it be such that if you let go of it, it will cost you so much.

David said, ***"…neither will I offer burnt offerings unto the LORD my God of that which doth cost me nothing."***

2 Sam. 24:24.

When what you HAVE is valuable, it will prosper you. God cannot lie. It will prosper your family. It will prosper your business.

"A man's gift maketh room for him, and bringeth him before great men."

Prov. 18:16.

The Hebrew word for **gift**, *mattan*, simply means a donation. Your gift has the capacity to create room for you. Have they told you that there is no vacancy? Take your gift to a man of God. Let him agree with you in prayers.

Let your gift create a room, a space, for you where you have been denied one.

Have they said that there is no accommodation for you? Let your gift make one for you. If God will have to remove somebody to put you, He will do it. He has done it before. He can do it again and again. Good news! He will do it for you!

One of my partner's baby was discovered to be a sickle cell carrier. She was devastated with the discovery. She and her husband kept it to themselves. She shared it with me and I asked her to plant a seed towards the miracle. She did. Some months later, there she was beaming with smiles that told me something good is happening. She first treated me to lunch and then shared the testimony. After some months, the doctors discovered that her blood has changed from sickle cell(SS) to AA. Wow! That is a miracle!

I want to challenge you to plant your seed today towards a miracle harvest. Some things will never change in your world until you plant a seed. There is a mighty harvest awaiting your response to this word today. You are just a step away from your harvest. That step is a seed. A miracle will settle your case!

Chapter Five

THE SECRET TO MIRACLES

There is a secret to miracles. As you know very well, secrets are always hidden, covered, veiled, and unknown until someone reveals them. One attribute of God is His ability to keep secrets. He is a specialist in the monopoly of divine secrets.

"The secret things belong unto the LORD our God: but those things which are revealed belong unto us and to our children for ever, that we may do all the words of this law."

Deut. 29:29.

There are several secrets that God has revealed unto us so that we can partake of His nature. He has revealed them unto us so that we can create our own miracles.

"At that time Jesus answered and said, I thank thee, O Father, Lord of heaven and earth, because thou hast hid these things from the wise and prudent, and hast revealed them unto babes."

Matt. 11:25.

The secret to working miracles is releasing what you HAVE to God and watch Him turn it to miracles of sort.

The principle is this: **loose what you HAVE to gain what you don't HAVE.**

Alternatively, gain what you Have to loose what you don't HAVE.

In life reverse is allowed. It is either you are progressing or you are retrogressing as long as you are in motion.

"...freely ye have received, freely give."

Matt. 10:8.

Be free in giving as much as you are free in receiving. How sad it is today that people clutch unto things as if they were born with them. Even if you were born with silver spoon in your mouth, somebody put that spoon there. You did not sweat for it. You received it freely. Now when there is a need for it, release it freely.

To gain you must give.

To receive you must release.

To harvest you must invest.

Nobody plants to fail. People just fail to plant.

Every farmer plants with expectation. There is an expected harvest that the farmer looks forward to. That is why he does not care so much about the labor he goes through.

"...who planteth a vineyard, and eateth not of the fruit thereof? Or who feedeth a flock, and eateth not of the milk of the flock?

.... he that ploweth should plow in hope; and that he that thresheth in hope should be partaker of his hope."

I Cor. 9:7,10.

"The husbandman that laboureth must be first partaker of the fruits."

2 Tim 2:6.

When the woman in our story released the pot of oil she had, God extended it. That one pot produced a harvest of many vessels of oil.

It will interest you to know that a seed can make a forest if it is planted.

In every seed there is a tree with fruits and more seeds. If you replant the seeds, then you will have more trees with more fruits and seeds. By the third planting, you can be sure of a forest. This is God's order.

"And God said, Let the earth bring forth grass, the herb yielding seed, and the fruit tree yielding fruit after his kind, whose seed is in itself, upon the earth: and it was so."

Gen.1:11.

For instance, in a seed of corn there are at least four cobs of corn with an average of one hundred seeds in each cob of corn. This one seed cannot satisfy you if you decide to eat it. When you plant it, it produces for you both seeds and fruit. Seeds for you to plant in order to ensure your next harvest season. Fruit for your next meal.

Anything that cannot meet your need is a seed. Learn to plant it. Discipline yourself to plant it.

Seeds are not meant to be eaten. They are meant to be planted.

You eat fruits not seeds. Only a foolish person will eat that one seed of corn just because they can't bear the pains of hunger.

The woman of Zarephath had one plate of food. Elijah said, ***"give it to me"***. Because he knew that it was not for her. I can now understand why he ate it with relish. He did not bother at all that the woman's son had not eaten. He knew that seeds are planted only fruits are to be eaten.

What is seed to you will be fruit to someone else other than you. The old adage says that one man's meat is another man's poison.

That reminds me of a story my friend told me. A man was relieved of his job when he least expected it. After a while of trying to survive, his family began to suffer hunger. One day they had just one meal for one person. So, his wife told him to eat it. For the life of him, it will be wicked to eat it when their only child was as hungry as himself and his wife.

He refused. His wife insisted that he should eat it. For the fact that she insisted, he ordered his wife to give it to their child instead. His wife refused.

Then she said that they wouldn't die if they don't eat besides it won't satisfy their hunger. Since he was going out to look for money that will bring more food, he should be the one to eat it. That makes sense.

You don't milk a cow that you have not fed. You don't harvest a farm that you have not planted.

If you want more, put in something that will get it.

A wise farmer will take one seed of corn and plant it. After three months, I believe, it will produce four cobs of corn with an average of four hundred seeds. Jesus said,

"Verily, verily, I say unto you, except a corn of wheat fall into the ground and die, it abideth alone: but if it die, it bringeth forth much fruit."

John 12:24.

Chapter Six

WALK IN WISDOM

The big question that you must answer now is: will you be wise to release that seed in your hand to God? Not because He needs it really. But for the fact that that is the raw material He needs to process your miracle.

The woman was bold and wise to release that single pot of oil. She harvested many vessels of oil in return that helped her to meet her needs. She was able to answer the creditor and her family lived on the proceed for the rest of their lives.

This is where the children of this world become wiser than the children of the kingdom. The reason is that non-believers in Christ can go to any extent to make sacrifices that promises a fortune. They damn the consequences.

Before she met her needs there is something fantastic that this woman did. She went back to Elisha to receive further instructions. This is where some people either lose their miracle or never live in it. I know that if she was like some Nigerians, as soon as she saw the vessels of oil she will never remember the man of God until another trouble strikes.

I have seen how wicked men and women use men of God as shrines and idols. I call them wicked because their hearts are not right with God. All they look for are the miracles. They don't want the miracle worker because they simply don't want any commitment.

Anything that has a source can only be sustained by that source. It is a fixed law of life.

If God is your source, He alone can sustain you. He gave you that miracle; you can only keep it by Him. So, that makes it necessary for you to stay in fellowship with Him. Be like Mary who chose the one thing that is needful: sitting at the feet of the Master to learn His ways and words.

> *"And Jesus answered and said unto her, Martha, Martha, thou art careful and troubled about many things:*
>
> *But one thing is needful: and Mary hath chosen that good part, which shall not be taken away from her."*
>
> Luke10: 41,42.

Seek God and you will find Him.

If you forsake Him, He will forsake you as well. In fact, He will even cast you off. What a dangerous state to find yourself if God does cast you away! To cast means to violently spit you out of His world.

"… if thou seek him, he will be found of thee; but if thou forsake him, he will cast thee off for ever."

I Chron. 28:9.

"…the Lord is with you, while ye be with him; and if ye seek him, he will be found of you; but if ye forsake him, he will forsake you."

2 Chron. 15:2.

May this not be your case in Jesus name. Amen.

There are people today who are suffering simply because they have killed their source like the Israelites did. Peter told them:

I want to challenge you to look deep into your life. Have you killed the voice of God in your heart? Have you offended a man of God that Jehovah used to introduce you to wealth, fame, etc.? Go back to your source and make amendments. This may be the key to your miracle. Go back to that man of God that God used to bless you. Plant a dangerous seed into his life. By that I mean, sow into his life what will hurt you because that is what will cause the release you have been struggling to have.

Chapter Seven

INSTRUCTIONS THAT
BRING THE MIRACLES

Elisha's message to the woman was pointed and clear. He said, *"...Go, sell the oil, and pay thy debt, and live thou and thy children of the rest."* 2 Kings 4:7.

The first instruction is **GO!** That is a command. It simply means to take action or move.

Every miracle comes when there is movement.

In the beginning when the earth was without form, void and darkness permeated every vapor. It was so bad that if you had planted a seed on that earth, it would not grow. Life was static. In fact, there was no life. Nothing happened until the Spirit of God began to move upon the face of the waters. Gen.1: 2.

Movement is the first sign of life. Life begins with it. I still remember my Biology in high school. We were taught that the first sign or characteristic of any living thing is movement.

If you want a miracle, then you must move. The Spirit must move. Smith Wigglesworth said that if the Spirit does not move, move the Spirit. What movements have you been experiencing lately? Those are the signals that your miracle is around the corner waiting for you to take action.

At the pool of Siloam (Bethesda) were impotent folks, ***"...waiting for the moving of the water..."*** Jn. 5:3. They were waiting. Mike Murdock said, *no one makes progress waiting except they are waiting on the Lord.* Many times we wait for the moving of the Spirit. We sing, *'when the Spirit of the Lord moves upon my* *heart, I will dance...'* If the Spirit is not moving, move the Spirit. Move!

The instruction is clear: **GO!** He did not say to wait. The Spirit and the Word are one. If God tells you to get out of your kindred and native land like He told Abraham in Genesis 12. It is because He has made provision where He is sending you to. You will be stupid to linger where you are for even a second longer.

I know that somebody will say, but this is all I have got. You see, the moment God tells you to GO, He takes away all the help and assistance you used to enjoy where you are. When the brook dried up for Elijah, God told him to move. I Kings 17:1-9.

If Elijah had stayed any moment longer, he would have died of thirst and hunger.

Do not behave like Lot. When God said to Lot to get out of Sodom, the Bible said that he lingered. He even gave excuses. *"And Lot said unto them, Oh, not so, my Lord…"* Gen.19: 18.

Do not complain like the impotent man even when the miracle worker Jesus was the one talking to him.

"The impotent man answered him, Sir, I have no man…"

John 5:7.

God is saying: Go! You are saying: not so Lord. You are complaining I have no man. I have no godfather. I have no long leg. Shut your mouth and move!

Friend, it is time to take action. Pick up your bed and GO! Pick up your legs and walk.

You have been questioning the air for too long without any concrete answer.

Now, get up and GO!

You have been waiting for that letter for too long, get up and GO for it. If the mountain cannot move towards you, GO towards it. Many times we expect God to move when He is expecting us to move. Move towards God and He will move towards you.

"Draw nigh to God, and He will draw nigh to you..."

James4 :8.

Every time Jesus performed a miracle, He would tell the person to get up and do something. Many experienced their miracles as they went. The ten lepers experienced their miracles as they went.

The proof of your knowledge of God is in the actions you take. What actions will you take today towards the manifestation of your miracles?

"By smooth words he will turn to godlessness those who act wickedly toward the covenant, but the people who know their God will display strength and take action."

Daniel 11:32. (New American Standard Version).

The next instruction was: Sell the oil.

To sell means to give up for a price. It also means to find buyers or purchasers. Find a trade. That which you HAVE, no matter how small it is, put a price tag on it. Look for a buyer.

Always remember that you HAVE something that the world is craving for. The world is in total disarray today just because you have not released to it that which you HAVE by divine endowment.

"For the earnest expectation of the creature waiteth for the manifestation of the sons of God."

Rom. 8 :19.

You have ignored that which you HAVE for too long.

You can sell your old books.

You can sell your used clothes.

You can sell those used bottles that are making your room messy.

You can sell those useless papers in your house.

You will soon realize that nothing is useless. You are the one who has labeled them to be useless for all this time because you don't need them. To the man who needs them, they are not useless.

Sell the oil!

What is the oil in your hand? Oil is used for food, so it can be food. Go sell food! Food is a daily need for every human being. Start a small food business at your front yard. You can even deliver to single men and women who can't cook for themselves. Many busy people starve while working. Take the food to them in their office for an extra price. They will pay for it and you will be rich by this.

Oil is used for beautification. So, it can be anything that beautifies. Find a work that will beautify your environment. Look for something that will beautify your boss or neighbor. Think of anything that will beautify them that you can put a price tag on and exchange for money. A man heard the word from a preacher about God causing pure water out of the rock. Those two words, pure water, just glued to his heart. That was the revelation he needed. He received strength and began pure water business. He made millions out of that idea.

What can you do for your neighbor that will improve their health, increase their wealth, etc? What can you do for your community that will bring a new feeling of excitement? Think! That is your oil! Put a price tag on it. Look for a purchaser. Trade it.

The next instruction is: Pay thy debt.

Are you indebted to someone or an organization or an institution? You can pay your debt if you follow the first two instructions.

Whether you like it or not, you are a debtor. There is someone who needs your help. Someone needs your services. Someone needs to hear your voice. Someone needs to see you. Someone needs your touch. Someone needs your shoulder to cry on. You owe them a debt. Pay it! If you deprive them, life may not be exciting for them.

There are people you owe a simple debt of *'I'm sorry'*. It will make a world of difference for them. There are some you owe a debt of *'I love you'*. It will change their steps. There are some you owe a simple debt of *'well done'*. It will increase their output. Pay your debt!

Some men owe their wives a big kiss of appreciation. Some women owe their husbands an overwhelming welcome back home. Some parents owe their children a loving hug. Some employers owe their employees a big pat on the back by raising their salary. Pay your debt!

The final instruction is: Live of the rest!

Enjoy life. It is true that your past may be full of bad and bitter experiences. Put it behind and enjoy the sweetness of life.

A careless lover may have broken your heart. That is past. Love again. You may have been accidented in the past. Put it behind. Enjoy life.

You may have been dumped in the past. Put it behind. Live life again as though nothing had happened.

Enjoy Life!

At times we take life too seriously that we forget to smile. We forget to laugh. We even forget to cry. We forget to go to the beach. We forget to give ourselves a vacation. We forget to give ourselves special treats. Young lady, if no man takes you out, you take yourself out. Give yourself a treat. The first three letters of the word funeral is fun. Before they attend your funeral make sure you have had the fun out of your little life on earth. If you don't have fun while you are alive, those who attend your funeral will have the fun while you are in the casket. Enjoy your life!

Friend, slap yourself to a new life. Learn to laugh again. Learn to cry when you have to. It is true people say weeping is for women and children. Weeping is a tonic that is good for your soul. It seems to clear your mind. I enjoy it when I have to weep with my dear wife. It is soothing. It is refreshing. Try it!

Learn to say 'No' when you mean it. Later you can change it but say it.

The woman changed her story as she played her part in the processing of her miracle. You too must play your part to partake of your miracle. A miracle will settle your case!

WHY I CHOSE JESUS CHRIST?

Someone asked me many years ago, Mike, why did you accept Jesus Christ? I could have become an atheist, a Muslim, etc. Why Jesus Christ?

My answer to that question is for basically three reasons and the fourth one will blow your mind.

One, I accepted Jesus Christ because I needed a Father. A father is a life source. That means you came from him. According to the law of sustenance, you can only be sustained by your source. Fish came out of water and thus can only be sustained in a water environment. If you put it on land, no matter how nice looking, it will die in no distant time. I realized that God is my Source. I can only be sustained by Him. I discovered that I couldn't have a personal relationship with Him through any other one or way except through Jesus Christ. John 14:6. Acts 4:12.

Like a fish out of water in a land environment, you and I continue to struggle to survive until we reconnect with our natural habitat or source. This is God your Father. This happens only through Jesus Christ. You will never be fulfilled or become eternally relevant until you accept Jesus Christ into your heart as your personal Lord and Master. Then will you be able to connect with God your Source. Then will you know what it means to be sustained by the grace of God.

Two, I accepted Jesus Christ because I needed a friend. Man was designed to relate with his environment and people. Nobody can survive as an island. You will need friends in your life. For me, it is very easy to make friends. As I grew up, my life became messed up by the friends I had. Friends betrayed me. Some battered me. Yet some others left me each time after our relationship with bruises. The marks will always be there. It was my search unknown to me for the real friend that got me into such relationships. I did not know about the Friend that sticks closer than a brother. Proverbs 18:24.

Friends have scorned me like they did Job. Job's friends turned aside from him (Job 6:18). They laughed him to scorn (Job 12:4). He was such a laughing stock that his eyes poured out tears to God (Job 16:20). His kinfolks failed him. His friends forgot him (Job 19:14). I have been there.

I needed a friend who will love me the way I am. I found this Friend in Jesus. He is God who became Abraham's Friend (Gen. 18:17. 2 Chron. 20:7). What a Friend He was to Abraham that even when Abraham lied about his wife, God rebuked the king to restore Abraham's wife (Gen. 12:10-20. 20:1-18.). A true friend will be there for you in good times and bad ones. Jesus is the best Friend I have ever had in my life. (John 15:14).

You will never know a true friend outside of Jesus Christ. Your parents? Spouse? Relatives? Classmates? Colleagues? I chose Jesus Christ because He will be there for me all the time. He said so and I believe Him.

Three, I needed a future. Life is past, present and future. I have seen the past; it was both good and bad. I cannot do anything about it. It is gone forever. I failed in the past. I did all the bad things in the past. But it is gone leaving me with the consequences of my wrong choices and deeds. Now I am in the present. What can I do to make the difference for my future? This is what I am concerned with today. I discovered that it is only in Jesus Christ that His precious blood washes my past away. My today is secured with His ever-abiding presence because He is a very present help. My tomorrow is taken care of because He told me not to worry about it.

I have a beautiful future in Jesus Christ because of what He did for me at the cross. I sinned and deserved to die. He took my sins and died in my place. In exchange, He gave me His very life, abundant life.

The fourth reason is that He changed my life. Religion tries to change people by principles, philosophies and practices. But Jesus came into my life without Him putting any demands on me to do things to earn His forgiveness. All He asked from me was to believe and receive Him. I did and found that my life is just changing every day. When I started this journey, I did not look like what I am today. I am not the same every day. I can assure you that by tomorrow I will become better until the day when I shall be changed permanently at the sound of the trump of God. From that point, I will put on immortality and incorruption. Sin shall never have dominion over me for all eternity. Is this not the kind of life you really desire from the deepest part of your being?

Today, my friend, you must make up your mind to receive Jesus Christ or reject Him. It is your choice. If you want to choose Jesus Christ, it is easy. Just say out loud:

Jesus, I believe You came to this world because You love me. Your love constrained You to the cross where You died for my sins. Jesus, I believe. Come into my heart today. Wash me with Your precious blood. Make me a new person whose love and passion will be for You the rest of my life on earth. Jesus, You are the Lord of my life from this day forward. Thank You for saving me in Jesus name. Amen.

If you have prayed this prayer, do write me today and I will send you some materials to help you in this journey to become all that God has designed you to be.

PARTNER WITH US

When God gives one man a vision, it will require the participation of several others to fulfill that vision. No single individual can carry out God's vision because God gives according to His size. Anyone who tries to fulfill God's vision by themselves either will get frustrated or finished off. In 1989, God told Brother Mike, *'Son, take this gospel and miracle power of the living Christ to the nations – impacting lives and destinies with the WORD.'* Since then, that word has been the driving force to reaching 30 million souls in at least 50 nations.

"And they beckoned unto their partners, which were in the other ship, that they should come and help them. And they came, and filled both the ships, so that they began to sink." Luke 5:7.

Through this message, we are beckoning on you to come alongside with us through your support and partnership. Help us reach millions around the world. Help us to fill our boat with a massive harvest. The beauty of this partnership is that when you help us, our boat and your boat will be filled. Together, we shall have a net breaking and boat sinking harvest.

Three things you CAN do to help us:

1. You can PRAY. Zech. 10:1. Acts 4:28-30. Eph. 6:18-20. Your prayers travel faster than the speed of light. You can commit to pray for us on a regular basis.

2. You can PLANT your seed of any size. Your money or material seed is the mobile force that moves the gospel from person to person and place to place. Your money or material is YOU GOing places you may not have the chance to be physically. Give generously. You can give your offering and seeds with your credit or debit card with this email address: ***amamieye@yahoo.co.uk*** through

https://www.pay.google.com or MAWO account details:

GTBank account number 0038894924. If you are outside Nigeria, you can give through MoneyGram.com for free. GTBank accepts money through MoneyGram for free. Use it while the opportunity last.

In Nigeria, you can give by using your bank code as follows:

For offering, dial:
*bankcode*000*491+amount#

For tithes, dial: *bankcode*000*492+amount#

If you are using GTBank for instance, your bank code is 737, so you can dial:
*737*000*491+amount#

If you are in the United States of America, you can give your offering to Bank of America account number 0905418443. ABA Routing number is: 121000358.

With Zelle, send to: **amamieye@yahoo.co.uk**

If you are in the United Kingdom, you can give your offering to NatWest Bank account number 52344819. Sort code 602112.

3. You can PARTICIPATE with us as you join forces with us in any location near you. I look forward to see you as we gather together a net breaking and boat sinking harvest. Luke 5:7. If you hear a voice saying, ignore this message, just know that it is the old serpent from the Garden. Tell that voice to shut up because you are the sheep of Jesus and you only obey the voice of your Master Jesus Christ. John 10:27. Thank you very much for obeying His voice in your heart and for being a part of what God is doing with us around the nations.

FOR MORE INFORMATION

You can enjoy the anointed ministry of the author through the many books he has written, his powerful messages on audiotapes, video and compact dics. Also by radio, television and internet. Use the address available below.

If God has blessed you through this ministry, send in your testimony today. We like to read or hear from you what God has done through this ministry. Someone can be saved, healed, helped and lifted up by your testimony.

Send in your prayer requests as well. Our God answers prayers today and always.

Take a bold step to partner with us as we strive to fulfill the God given mandate to reach thirty million souls in at least fifty countries of the world within the shortest possible time and through every available means. You can make online donations through our secure and safe web site. You can use your credit or debit cards at any time.

You can also purchase our products online. Just log on today

For more spiritual help, counseling and prayer ministration, contact:

Bishop Michael O. Amamieye

Michael Amamieye Word Outreach International

a/k/a Aggressive Faith Ministries

Plot 13 Walter Akpana Lay Out

Off 394 Ikwerre Road Mile 5 Rumueprikom

P. O. Box 12378, Port Harcourt, Nigeria.

Phone: +234-901800MAWO (Nigeria); +1-916-245-6157(U.S.A.)

E-mail: info@aggressivefaith.org

Web site: www.aggressivefaith.org

ABOUT THE AUTHOR

Psalm 40:2,3 is a keynote to the life and ministry of Michael O. Amamieye. He was radically saved, healed and delivered from the power of darkness that endangered his youth. He is a living proof of God's matchless and abundant grace.

Since 1983, Brother Mike has been president, pastor and pioneer of several fellowships, churches and movements. He is instrumental in birthing many sons and daughters unto glory. He is a consecrated bishop with an oversight that reaches five continents.

In 1984, the Lord called Brother Mike to world evangelism with a mandate to *take the gospel and miracle power of the risen Christ to the nations – impacting lives and destinies with the WORD!* He is the President of **Michael**

Amamieye Word Outreach International *also known as* **Aggressive Faith Ministries** with headquarters in the Garden City of Port Harcourt, Nigeria. He is the President of **Intensive Ministers Training School**. He is the Chairman of **Aggressive Faith Publishing Company**. Through this ministry, Brother Mike is determined to reach at least thirty million souls in at least fifty nations with the simple proclamation of the gospel of Christ with evidence that brings salvation, healing, deliverance, blessing and joy.

An evangelist by calling, he is a graduate of the **Billy Graham School of Evangelism**. He is a member of **Proclamation Evangelism Network** and an associate evangelist with the **Global Network of Evangelists** founded by the **Luis Palau Association**. He has been interviewed on **Decision Today** Radio broadcast and **Decision** magazine both of which are owned by the **Billy Graham Evangelistic Association.** He has also appeared on GODTV as well as several other networks around the world.

Bishop Mike is a member of the **International Communion of Charismatic Churches** founded by the late Archbishop Benson Idahosa and several others. He has been honored in a public ceremony where the Mayor of the city of East Cleveland, Ohio gave him the key to the city in 2003. **LEADS Africa** honored him as an icon of nation building in 2012. **The Voice** magazine in Holland honored him with the spiritual leadership award in 2014. In 2019, he was awarded an honorary doctorate degree by **Triune Biblical University** in New York. He is on high demand in crusades, conferences and conventions around the world.

He is the author of more than twenty books. He is a prolific and thought captivating writer with many of his works published in newsletters, magazines and newspapers around the world.

Bishop Mike is happily married to Princess Monivi, an ordained minister of the gospel and a health consultant. They are blessed with two biological children, Edwina Aleme and Mehetabel Favour as well as many others.